West Country Verses Vol I

Edited by Jessica Woodbridge

First published in Great Britain in 2006 by:
Young Writers
Remus House
Coltsfoot Drive
Peterborough
PE2 9JX
Telephone: 01733 890066
Website: www.youngwriters.co.uk

SB ISBN 1 84602 637 7

Foreword

Young Writers was established in 1991 and has been passionately devoted to the promotion of reading and writing in children and young adults ever since. The quest continues today. Young Writers remains as committed to the nurturing of poetic and literary talent as ever.

This year's Young Writers competition has proven as vibrant and dynamic as ever and we are delighted to present a showcase of the best poetry from across the UK and in some cases overseas. Each poem has been selected from a wealth of *A Pocketful Of Rhyme* entries before ultimately being published in this, our fourteenth primary school poetry series.

Once again, we have been supremely impressed by the overall quality of the entries we have received. The imagination, energy and creativity which has gone into each young writer's entry made choosing the poems a challenging and often difficult but ultimately hugely rewarding task - the general high standard of the work submitted ensured this opportunity to bring their poetry to a larger appreciative audience.

We sincerely hope you are pleased with this final collection and that you will enjoy *A Pocketful Of Rhyme West Country Verses Vol I* for many years to come.

Contents

The Poems

Natural Colours

What is white?
Soft waves rolling in, all frothy like coffee
Silent ripples, all clear
Sometimes big or sometimes small
But not always frothy.

What is black?
A swan with wings of jet-black
Sliding with the other tired swans that have come
To the beautiful lake for the winter
Where in the north, it is cold.

What is copper?
A red squirrel all fluffy, running as if
Dancing through the undergrowth
Up in a tree, down on the ground
But always gathering nuts.

What is pink?
Clouds still in an evening sky, pink and fluffy
In the west, but dark on the other side
When the sun goes down.

Nathan Williams (9)
Blaise Primary School, Bristol

Colours

What is blue?
A certificate that hangs on the wall
It has no movement at all
It might fall now and again
The wall keeps it there
The children win it.

What is white?
A whiteboard with teacher's writing all over it
What keeps it there?
With a lovely pale green border
The teacher puts what they have to do on it.

What is green?
A crispy crunchy leaf that hangs on the tree
When the leaf falls it turns brown.

James Gibbs (10)
Blaise Primary School, Bristol

What Is?

What is pink?
Why a graceful flamingo standing proud on his elegant legs
All pink with fluffy feathers
He stands in the aqua, crystal clear river.

What is purple?
Why a purple elegant dress that a golden girl wears
All day long, 24/7 in the purple night.

What is red?
Why a ruby ring on a red-breasted robin
She wears on her brown wing
Who gave the ruby ring to the red robin?

What is gold?
Why a tall golden girl with golden shining hair
A golden dress and a golden stone cottage.

What is white?
Why an elegant swan floating on the crystal clear river
Dipping her head under the shimmering water.

Karli Thomas-Walker (10)
Blaise Primary School, Bristol

Colours All Around Us

What is yellow?
The swaying wind makes the sand
Go from side to side and up and down
It is silent, but plays with the sea
The sea gathers the sand
Makes it soggy, not very nice.

What is blue?
The sea may look silent
But as soon as you go into the sea
The sea comes to life
The fish are dancing and having fun
They enjoy being underwater.

What is brown?
The galloping horse is jumping up and down
With his solid horseshoes clicking and clacking up and down the road
They sometimes hop and gallop along the road.

What is blue and red?
The fish-eating kingfisher is gliding down into the crystal clear river
Gathering fish for his children
The colourful kingfisher is taking its children out to catch the food.

Alistair Dorney (9)
Blaise Primary School, Bristol

Why I Didn't Go Swimming

I didn't go swimming,
I didn't go swimming because I didn't have a swimming kit
I didn't have a swimming kit because I was in a rush this morning
I was in a rush this morning because I stayed in bed too late
I stayed in bed too late because I watched a film
I watched a film because I was bored
I was bored because there was nothing to do
And that is my excuse.

Amy Thornhill (9)
Blaise Primary School, Bristol

School Is Over

School is over
There's things to do
Instead of doing homework all day through
I sit at home all the time
My mum tells me to go to the washing line.

Maisie Atwill (9)
Blaise Primary School, Bristol

What Colours Are In The World?

What is white?
A white, fluffy, huge polar bear
Stomping loudly around with his shining thick fur
Swaying from side to side.

What is gold?
A golden fireball of sun
Beaming on you like an alarm
The beams are fast and furious.

What is red?
A shiny, tiny, glistening ant
Scurrying around worriedly
Carrying his bundle of food
With all his strength and might.

What is blue?
A swaying, sparkling, crystal clear river
Flowing softly
Making a glistening face as it sails softly away.

Alannah Meechan (10)
Blaise Primary School, Bristol

Colours

What is pink?
A graceful flamingo standing elegantly
On one pole-like leg
In a crystal clear river
Fluttering his soft beautiful feathers.

What is red?
A gorgeous scented rose
Glistening like a million stars in the sunshine
As it sways to and fro
In the gentle breeze.

What is white?
A fluffy dream-like cloud
Floating around in the baby-blue sky
As it slowly and softly
Drifts to a heavenly sleep.

What is yellow?
A sun like a shining hot ball of gold
Glistening in the sky
Beaming down like a slash of light
The powerful leader orders the clouds to dance.

Lauren Thomas (10)
Blaise Primary School, Bristol

Colours

What is green?
Apple-green grass
Shining in the sunlight
With the dark emerald-green bushes
Sat on the lovely green grass.

What is white?
The glistening snow shining bright
The crystal clear snow
Slowly changing into a soggy brown
As children step upon it.

What is blue?
A bright cornflower
Glistening in the golden sun
Bright as can be the cornflower shall be.

What is violet?
Clouds are violet in the summer twilight
Swooshing through the sparkling sky.

Esmé McCrum (10)
Blaise Primary School, Bristol

Colours

What is green?
A bright green leaf
Falls out of the old oak tree
It touches the soft green grass.

What is red?
A glittering ruby
It shines as it catches the sun.

What is yellow?
The shimmering sun is like a ball of gold
It never dies down
Forever it gives us light.

What is blue?
A bouncy ball
It bounces so far
It almost reaches to the stars.

What is orange?
An orange is orange
And that is it.

Lauren Fifield (10)
Blaise Primary School, Bristol

Colours Of The Rainbow

What is yellow?
The sand is yellow
Brightly coloured it feels nice and soft
When it gets between your toes it feels really bitty.

What is blue?
The sea is blue
Swishing from side to side
Splashing on the rocks.

What is green?
Grass is green blowing in the wind
Growing new flowers day by day
It will grow and grow.

What is brown?
Mud is brown with pigs bathing in it
Animals getting very muddy
When playing in it.

Cheyanne Lovell (10)
Blaise Primary School, Bristol

Colours

What is white?
A peaceful duck waddling along
The rich bright green grass.

What is yellow?
A bright sun swaying backwards and forwards
In the bright blue sky.

What is blue?
A calm and quiet sea
Crystal clear with a bright orange fish
Swimming and dashing around.

What is green?
A calm, quiet, swaying patch of rich golden grass.

Marley Rugman (10)
Blaise Primary School, Bristol

Colours

What is red?
A crab walking sideways on the sandy beach
Trying to catch his tea, pinching the air.

What is white?
A peaceful horse galloping in soggy mud
Getting his backside covered in dark mud.

What is silver?
A shiny space rocket
Just about to blast up into the starry night.

What is pink?
A flamingo standing on one twig-like leg
In a steady, dark, blue river
Trying to catch his slippery food.

Ashley Saunders (9)
Blaise Primary School, Bristol

Colours Of The Rainbow

What is red?
A swaying ruby poppy blowing in the breeze
Sitting by a crystal clear lake
The golden sun shining with people having a picnic
Sat next to the red, red ruby of the apple-green grass.

What is white?
A snow-white swan gliding in the clear sparkling river
A golden-yellow beak on the pure white feathers
of the snow-white swan.

What is green?
The shining emerald apple hanging from the light brown branches
Of the big oak tree wobbling in the breeze.

What is blue?
A crystal clear topaz sky
With clouds the shape of animals blowing gently in the breeze.

Kim Moss (9)
Blaise Primary School, Bristol

Colours

What is pink?
A peaceful flamingo silently standing on one fine strong leg
In a sparkling river sleeping with bushy feathers tucked behind him.

What is red?
A poppy's red, red and blowing in the breeze
Petals falling to the ground.

What is blue?
Crystal clear water is blue
Swishing and swooshing in the wind as the leaves fall in.

What is white?
A beautiful swan is white
Floating as it dashes in the sparkling lake.

What is purple?
An amethyst is purple
Gleaming in the moonlight twilight.

Chloe Roberts (9)
Blaise Primary School, Bristol

Colours In The Garden

What is blue?
Blue is a painted blue chair on the carpet
Making the blue alien sit on it.

What is white?
School T-shirt is white,
Double glazed windows flying on the white clouds.

What is yellow?
Painted walls gleaming against yellow posters.

What is black?
Black shiny sky
Black is me walking in the streets.

Jai Webster Lewis (10)
Blaise Primary School, Bristol

Rainbow Colours

What is red?
Fire burning down the town.

What is yellow?
Daffodils swaying in the breeze.

What is pink?
The sky in the waves of the wind.

What is blue?
The sea swaying in the deep.

What is white?
Doves flying high in the sky.

Conor Cooke (9)
Blaise Primary School, Bristol

Rainbows Of The World

What is red?
A small greedy crab running sideways
To catch his frightened prey is red.

What is green?
A field of growing grass blowing in the cold, cold, breezy night
With sparkly and shining glory.

What is blue?
A big, square, double glazed window is blue
For me to look quietly through.

What is pink?
A sunset is pink up high in the night sky
With sparkly stars starting to awaken, opening a new adventure.

Eleanor Maggs (9)
Blaise Primary School, Bristol

What Is?

What is pink?
Why a graceful flamingo standing proud on his thin, strong,
twig-like legs
With its head in the crystal clear water hunting for juicy fish.

What is red?
Why a rose is red blowing in the breeze
Petals falling to the ground standing and swaying
in-between the green.

What is white?
Why a beautiful swan is white
Floating on the aqua-clear water as it sings.

What is yellow?
Why the beautiful shining sun is yellow
Giving us light in the day to see our way.

What is gold?
A golden girl's hair is shining in the golden light
Swishing and swooshing in the wind.

Hannah Oxenham (9)
Blaise Primary School, Bristol

The Stone Brothers

What is red?
Rubies are red
A ruby that gleams in the bright beams.

What is blue?
Sapphire is blue
A sapphire that is dark and glows gracefully in the light but still dark.

What is green?
Emeralds are green being searched for
It's a beautiful bright green that glitters and gleams.

What is purple?
An amethyst is purple
Shining gracefully awaiting the miner's face.

Declan Stinchcombe (10)
Blaise Primary School, Bristol

The Stone Brothers

What is green?
Emerald glistening green stone
Emerald is green glowing in the dark
Staying there with two brothers
Ruby and sapphire they are.

What is red?
A shining red ruby
What is red?
A sparkling red ruby gleaming in the dark
Valuable to most people as it shines with red sparks.

What is blue?
A little shining sapphire
What is blue?
Sapphire is blue shining with great pride
With his brothers two sold at a very high price.

What is purple?
Gems are purple
What is purple?
Gems are purple shining so gracefully
Awaiting to be mined, sparkling purple are thee.

Luke Dodd (9)
Blaise Primary School, Bristol

Colours

What is pink?
A gentle flamingo standing quietly on one thin leg
In a flowing pond waiting for pink shrimp.

What is yellow?
A glittering sun like a ball of shimmering gold
Up in the sky so high.

What is red?
A noisy car
Brmm, brmm, as it goes by.

What is blue?
The shimmering sea
A little boat floating about, little fishes dancing about.

What is silver?
The glowing stars
That come out at night.

Ashleigh Mathias (10)
Blaise Primary School, Bristol

Colours Of The Rainbow

What is pink?
A peaceful flamingo standing on one weak lanky leg
In a sparkling white lake, chomping on shiny shrimps.

What is white?
A sparkling swan by a crystal white lake
A golden yellow beak nibbling on a sweet-smelling rose.

What is red?
A ruby-red poppy, smooth as your touch
The petals smelling sweet as a rose.

What is green?
A sparkly crocodile with white shining teeth
Swimming in the dark muddy lake.

What is yellow?
A great ball of gold
With the golden sun glistening out.

Georgia Smith (10)
Blaise Primary School, Bristol

Beautiful Rainbow Colours

What is gold?
Spring leaves are gold
Just lying on a brown branch beginning to unfold.

What is white?
White is a bunny eating a rose that's pink
Sitting by a bush nearby having a peaceful drink.

Anna Watts (9)
Blaise Primary School, Bristol

The Rainbow Colours

What is blue?
A round small blueberry on a small bright green bush in the wind.

What is green?
A round big apple on a big light green tree still in the lovely
hot summer.

What is yellow?
A big, round, juicy watermelon.

What is red?
A small juicy raspberry.

Mazhabin Ali (10)
Blaise Primary School, Bristol

An Aeroplane

An aeroplane was flying, flying high in the sky
The plane did a somersault
The plane went down onto the runway
It took off again
The plane did another somersault
Then the plane landed.

Scott Everett (9)
Blaise Primary School, Bristol

My Puppy Piper

My puppy Piper smells of garden grass
She always makes me laugh
She really hates baths
She always splashes around
She loves her little ball
She acts like she's very cool
She loves playing with me
I love playing with her
My puppy Piper.

Jordan Webber (10)
Blaise Primary School, Bristol

About School

S pelling is fun
C atch the ball
H omework is finished
O utside games with friends
O pen your school bag
L ate for class.

Chantelle Kyokutmba (9)
Blaise Primary School, Bristol

My Sweet Shop

When I own a sweet shop
I want lots of sweets for customers and me
I want fizz bombs which make your mouth go on fire
You should know now about my sweet shop
When I own a sweet shop
I want lots of sweets for customers and me
I hope my customers like my sweet shop
Because it is new and the only sweet shop in Birmingham.

Samantha Robertson (9)
Blaise Primary School, Bristol

Summer

S ummer is here
U nhappy children turning happy
M ornings when I wake up, birds begin to sing
M ake cold drinks and have fun
E very day when I get up
R unning to the window, it's sunny.

Leah Evans (9)
Blaise Primary School, Bristol

Chocolate

C hocolate can be milk, plain or white
H ot chocolate is great
O r lovely with cream and marshmallows
C hocolate, chocolate
O h how lovely you are
L ittle squares of chocolate
A t midnight for a snack
T ake a break at midnight
E at that lovely chocolate.

James Vickery (9)
Blaise Primary School, Bristol

Dolphins

Dolphins swimming in the night
Water splashing, turning white.

All the fish swim away
So they're not a dolphin's meal today.

All the dolphins come out to play
Always having lots to say.

Dolphins jumping really high
Looks like they're flying in the sky.

As the sailors sail by
The dolphins always wink their eye.

If you have ever seen a dolphin swim far away
I wish I could see a dolphin today.

Carlsharee Rodway (10)
Blaise Primary School, Bristol

Sweets

S weets can make your teeth fall out
W e believe that they can fall out in a month
E veryone used to have sweets
E veryone in the shops has sweets
T aste sweets and have some now
S weets are very unhealthy and make you fat.

Alex Whitmarsh (9)
Blaise Primary School, Bristol

Myself

Here I am, looking at me
Here he is, coming towards me
He is there
I am here
We are thinking about the fair.

We're on the rides having fun
I cannot stand that boiling sun
Time to get off
The rides are closing
The sun has gone, time for dozing.

Alex Groves (9)
Blaise Primary School, Bristol

Kitty Baby

Don't leave your kitty baby
Sitting by the cave
A bear might eat her
Yum, yum, yum.

Don't leave your kitty baby
Sitting by the hill
A hare might chase her
Hop, hop, hop.

Don't leave your kitty baby
Walking on the street
A dog might bite her
Bark, bark, bark.

Keep your kitty baby
Feed her on fresh milk
Help arrange her Whiskas
Miaow, miaow, miaow.

Ricky Yip (10)
Blaise Primary School, Bristol

Myself

I look in the mirror and what do I see?
Big brown eyes staring at me!

Hair put back straight, black as can be
Teeth straight and shiny, I don't mind being me.

I look in the mirror and what do I see?
I see myself staring at me.

Maaya Pandit (10)
Blaise Primary School, Bristol

Me And Myself

I look in the mirror and what do I see?
My big sister staring at me
We both have dark hair and green, green eyes
Tiny pink ears
I can't stand the tears
I am smiling with big red cheers
Lovely white teeth
Sweet and shining.

Emily Stone (8)
Blaise Primary School, Bristol

Reflection

I look in the mirror and what do I see?
I see my reflection looking at me.

I put up my hand and what do I see?
I see my reflection, it's copying me.

I look in the mirror and what do I see?
I see my reflection smiling at me.

I look in the mirror and what do I see?
I see my reflection, it's the same as me.

Tilly Lewis (9)
Blaise Primary School, Bristol

Walking Through The Jungle

Walking through the jungle, what did I see?
A big dirty elephant stamping on me.

Walking through the jungle, what did I see
A stripy scary tiger charging after me.

Walking through the jungle, what did I see?
A little cheeky monkey crying for his tea.

Walking through the jungle, what did I see?
A pathway home only for me.

Usha Ali (7)
Blaise Primary School, Bristol

Walking Through The Jungle

Walking through the jungle, what did I see?
A big hairy lion sprinting after me.

Walking through the jungle, what did I see?
A big scary rhino fast asleep.

Walking through the jungle, what did I see?
A hairy funny monkey taking the mick out of me.

Walking through the jungle, what did I see?
An enormous grey elephant stamping after me.

Walking through the jungle, what did I see?
A green slithery snake chasing me.

Walking through the jungle, what did I see?
A fast place out just for me.

Kieran Lovell (8)
Blaise Primary School, Bristol

Farmyard Poem

Walking through the farmyard, what did I see?
A big fat cow coming for me.

Walking through the farmyard, what did I see?
A pink lazy pig oinking at me.

Walking through the farmyard, what did I see?
A big brown bull charging at me.

Walking through the farmyard, what did I see?
A big red tractor chasing after me.

Carrie Fitzgerald (7)
Blaise Primary School, Bristol

Walking Through The Jungle

Walking through the jungle what did I see?
A hungry stripy tiger roaring at me.

Walking through the jungle what did I see?
A grey muddy elephant charging at me.

Walking through the jungle what did I see?
A big hairy gorilla running after me.

Walking through the jungle what did I see?
A round fat hippo laughing at me.

Walking through the jungle what did I see?
A big fat monkey drinking his tea.

Walking through the jungle what did I see?
A path to safety, just for me.

Gemma Fay (8)
Blaise Primary School, Bristol

Walking Through The Jungle

Walking through the jungle what did I see?
A fat jumping bear staring at me.

Walking though the jungle what did I see?
I saw a wild cat attacking me.

Walking through the jungle what did I see?
A grey hippo running at me.

Walking through the jungle what did I see?
A running rhino charging at me.

Walking through the jungle what did I see?
An annoying parrot talking to me.

Matthew Masters (8)
Blaise Primary School, Bristol

Walking Through The Jungle

Walking through the jungle what did I see?
A green and yellow snake hissing at me.

Walking through the jungle what did I see?
A hungry alligator watching me.

Walking through the jungle what did I see?
A brown monkey laughing at me.

Walking through the jungle what did I see?
A big grey hippopotamus blowing bubbles at me.

Stacey Barrett (8)
Blaise Primary School, Bristol

Walking Through The Jungle

Walking through the jungle, what did I see?
A jumpy spider jumping at me.

Walking through the jungle, what did I see?
A baby pink ostrich sitting by the water.

Walking through the jungle, what did I see?
A little baby monkey hanging on the tree.

Walking through the jungle, what did I see?
A big hairy lion sprinting after me.

Rhys Gibbs (8)
Blaise Primary School, Bristol

Street Poems

Walking through the street what can I see?
My dad shopping for me.

Walking through the street what can I see?
A big cat sitting on the wall by me.

Walking through the street what can I see?
A dog barking at me.

Walking through the street what can I see?
Two dogs biting me.

Walking through the street what can I see?
A big bike cycling down the road after me.

Walking through the street what can I see?
My parents waiting for me.

Walking through the street what can I see?
My nan waiting for me.

Walking through the street what can I see?
A baby in a pushchair staring at me.

Walking through the street what can I see?
A bunch of children playing with me.

Walking through the street what can I see?
A big cool Lamborghini racing me.

Walking through the street what can I see?
A baby winking at me.

Walking through the street what can I see?
A big aeroplane flying in the sky.

Walking through the street what can I see?
A big fat horse trotting down the road.

Walking through the street what can I see?
A big fat car going down the road after me.

Liam Lloyd (8)
Blaise Primary School, Bristol

My Winter Poem

You can tell it's winter
When snowflakes drop like a splinter.
When you go out the snow is like a white blanket cover.

You can tell it's winter
Because it'll be dark like the night
You can have a snowball fight.

You can hear the snowflakes hit the snow
You can have a log fire with your own dog.

Ashley Miles (8)
Blaise Primary School, Bristol

Walking Through The Jungle

Walking through the jungle, what did I see?
A large grey elephant charging at me.

Walking through the jungle, what did I see?
A big gorilla roaring at me.

Walking through the jungle, what did I see?
A fat furry bear glaring at me.

Walking through the jungle, what did I see?
An arrow pointing the way.

Kaylan Usherwood (8)
Blaise Primary School, Bristol

Walking Through The Farmyard

Down at the farmyard, what can I see?
A big fat bull charging at me.

Down at the farmyard, what can I see?
A white round cow striding at me.

Down at the farmyard, what can I see?
A white baby sheep bleating at me.

Down at the farmyard, what can I see?
A big brown horse galloping towards me.

Down at the farmyard, what can I see?
My mum and dad waiting for me.

Georgia Thomas (7)
Blaise Primary School, Bristol

Walking Through The Jungle

Walking through the jungle what did I see?
A beautiful butterfly staring at me.

Walking through the jungle what did I see?
A lovely cat purring at me.

Walking through the jungle what did I see?
A nice giraffe glaring at me.

Walking through the jungle what did I see?
A cheeky monkey taking a picture of me.

Walking through the jungle what did I see?
My mum and dad waiting for me.

Freya Rose (7)
Blaise Primary School, Bristol

Farmyard Poem

Walking through the farmyard, what did I see?
A horrible mean goat chasing after me.

Walking through the farmyard, what did I see?
A lazy cow mooing at me.

Walking through the farmyard, what did I see?
A big fat chicken flying over me.

Walking through the farmyard, what did I see?
A big pink pig oinking at me.

Walking through the farmyard, what did I see?
My mum and dad waiting for me.

Robyn Nichols (8)
Blaise Primary School, Bristol

Walking Through The Farmyard

Walking through the farmyard what did I see?
A big fat bull charging at me.

Walking through the farmyard what did I see?
A white and black cow striding at me.

Walking through the farmyard what did I see?
A big brown horse galloping at me.

Walking through the farmyard what did I see?
My mum and dad waiting for me.

Kelsea Mallinson (8)
Blaise Primary School, Bristol

Walking Through The Jungle

Walking through the jungle what did I see?
A large grey elephant charging at me.

Walking through the jungle what did I see?
A butterfly laughing at me.

Walking through the jungle what did I see?
A spider crawling on me.

Walking through the jungle what did I see?
An owl hooting at me.

Walking through the jungle what did I see?
An elephant stamping on me.

Charlie Turnbull (9)
Blaise Primary School, Bristol

Banana

B ananas taste good
A s nice as can be
N o other fruit can taste like this
A banana is so nice
N o fruit can beat it
A lways taste so good.

Rebecca Bennett (11)
Holymead Junior School, Bristol

School

S it down, now!
C hewing gum out of your mouth!
H omework must be in by tomorrow
O K Miss, yes Miss.
O K, you may leave the room but . . .
L eave silently.

Hannah Smith (11)
Holymead Junior School, Bristol

Winter

Snowflakes are falling
They melt on the ground
Mist is growing
There's fog all around.

Robins are singing
They need lots to eat
They hop around
On two tiny feet.

It's winter, it's winter
Come join the fun
Giving and sharing
The season's begun.

Bethany Jennings (11)
Holymead Junior School, Bristol

Dolphins

D usky dolphins
O ver the world you can find them
L ittle, big, whatever size and shape
P layful
H uman friendly
I ntelligent creatures
N ever travel on their own.

Nicole Hunt (11)
Holymead Junior School, Bristol

Summer

The sizzling summer sun is very hot
Burning you red on the spot
Noisy children play on the beach
While lazy adults sunbathe in the heat.

Dehydrating plants dying in the heat
Barbecues, many people wanting to eat
Drought, sand, no water to drink
Sunbathing floaters begin to sink.

Everyone outside laughing and joking
Young children with sticks are a-poking
Rain sometimes, but mostly sun
Everyone's having fun!

Katie Cook (11)
Holymead Junior School, Bristol

Baby Sister

B ig eyes
A noisy mouth
B ig bum
Y our silly smile

S miley, fun, enjoyable
I ncredibly cute
S o small
T oo cuddly
E xtremely brown hair
R eally fun sister.

Hannah Loving (11)
Holymead Junior School, Bristol

Weather Race

Whilst the mad wind runs
The sun skips ahead
Then the rain falls down
And the sun leads ahead
The race is tough
The race is mean
They all run across the blue
Highlighted sky
The white fluffy clouds get
Blown out the way, the greatest
Of all, the sun
Wins the race *again!*

Paige Edgell (10)
Holymead Junior School, Bristol

Frankenstein School

Thud, thud, thud down the hall
The creak of a door, the squeak of a mouse
Singing in the distance, the laughter of children
No one's here, school is out.

Thump, thump, thump in the classroom
The wind through the window, the blowing of curtains
The chirping of the birds, the barks of dogs,
No one's here, school is out.

Bang, bang, bang in the library
The rustle of paper, the murmur of reading
The zip of a school bag, the purr of a cat
No one's here, school is out.

There's never children running through the school
It's been abandoned for years now
There's never the smile of children to lighten up the day
Or the chatter in the hall as they run around the school.

The ghost of the past is haunting
Making the noises of the school children
There is no one around to hear it
For this is Frankenstein school.

Alice Gregory (11)
Holymead Junior School, Bristol

A Scary Creature

V ery frightening like the dark
A s furry as a feather
M unches on blood
P retty, tiny and small
I nteresting and shiny fangs
R eally silky and smooth cape
E veryone knows her name
S he is Vampire teddy!

Megan Bowell (11)
Holymead Junior School, Bristol

You!

You're just like the burning sun,
With your warm loving smile
And not a single bad thought on your mind.

You're just like a glowing star
Always shining down on people when they're sad, upset
or even devastated
And a mind of your own.

You're just like an amazing angel
Everyone loves you
And could never ever let you down.

You,
You are just what everyone wants to be
The only reason ever that someone could hate you is
That they want to be just like you!

You're everyone's sun, star and angel
And that's all you'll ever be
Nothing more, nothing less
But everyone loves you so!

Abigail Batt (11)
Holymead Junior School, Bristol

The World

The world is such a special place,
It always puts a smile on my face,
The birds, the flowers and the trees
And even insects like bumblebees.
The world is a special place,
it should put a smile on everybody's face.

Georgina Godfrey (11)
Holymead Junior School, Bristol

No More Mr Nice Guy!

Do your homework!
Finish your test!
Remember your PE kit!
Sit at your desk!
I never want to do these things at school, but . . .

Sharpen those pencils!
Hand in your dinner money!
Write a poem!
It isn't that funny!

No more Mr Nice Guy!
But I suppose, the teacher knows best!

Becky Payne (11)
Holymead Junior School, Bristol

World Cup Fever

W orld Cup is going to be yours England
O wen, boot the ball up there
R obinson, don't let a goal in
L ampard, do your loony stuff
D avid Beckham play your shots

C ome on England you can do it
U p you get Wayne Rooney and do your scoring
P eter Crouch, do your scoring

F orever, now England the trophy is yours
E very game you will win
V ery good England, now off you go
E ven you could beat anyone
R ooney is your name but football is your game.

Ruby Harrison (7)
Ilfracombe CE Junior School, Ilfracombe

World Cup Fever

W icked way to go England
O wen give it a shot
R ooney get extra better
L ampard do your best in the middle
D avid Beckham do your best

C ome on England cry your tears out
U p you get England go on win the match
P eter Crouch defends well

F orever the trophy might be yours England, England, England
E very time the trophy will be yours
V ery good luck to England
E verything you do you will win
R ooney, now off you go to the pitch.

Chloe James (7)
Ilfracombe CE Junior School, Ilfracombe

World Cup Fever

W e are at the World Cup stadium
O wen you can score a goal
R ooney is your foot OK?
L isten to the fans scream and shout, 'Come on England.'
D o your best for the England fans

C ome on England, you can win
U kraine you can beat
P ut your effort into it

F ootball is the best
E very day work hard
V ery mind taking
E verybody in my family is excited
R ooney, Peter Crouch and Owen deserve a medal!

Kira Chew
Ilfracombe CE Junior School, Ilfracombe

World Cup Fever

W e are counting on you
O nly three days to go
R ooney, Rooney hope you feel better
L ight up the England team
D on't give up England

C arry on all the way
U se all your best players
P lay your best

F ans are going wild
E ngland show them who's boss
V ote for England, they are the best
E ven the best teams are nothing compared to you
R isk against Germany!

Archie Williams-Mills (8)
Ilfracombe CE Junior School, Ilfracombe

World Cup Fever

W ow! England win this for us
O ur country's counting on you
R ead your heart that you can do this
L et yourself win
D on't let your country down now

C ome on England, don't let us down
U p you go if you win this now
P eople are going crazy don't give up now

F inish this game for us
E ven your team is counting on us
V ictory is trying to win the game
E ven we're counting on you
R each for that trophy.

Charlotte Calvert
Ilfracombe CE Junior School, Ilfracombe

World Cup Fever

W orld Cup here we come
O h don't let us down now England
R ipped off his shirt he scored a goal
L ions are cheering
D efeat the opposition

C an we do it?
U se your feet Owen
P eople want you to win

F ootball
E verybody loves you
V ictory is waiting
E veryone's cheering for you
R ooney win!

Nadia Shergold (8)
Ilfracombe CE Junior School, Ilfracombe

World Cup Fever

W ow, England have qualified
O wen headed it in
R un Walcott and score
L ose and it's all over
D on't back down

C ome on England
U p the ball goes to Lampard
P ut on your boots and play your best

F inally England have won
E veryone is watching around the world
V ery good match England
E ngland score the penalty
R obbo punch that ball out of the box.

Daniel Hall
Ilfracombe CE Junior School, Ilfracombe

World Cup Fever

W icked England are going to cheer us on
O ver all countries, England is definitely best
R ooney you just have to make us win
L ooking and cheering fans - that makes England better
D reading versus Germany

C atching the ball off another player's shot
U h oh, why tackle the ball off me?
P utting up with a bleeding knee to win the cup - victory's
a second away

F ighting for the *abb!* Nooo
E veryone's shaking
V s millions of teams we could easily win
E ngland's in the lead - to nothing
R eally sweaty and hot - but I'd better shoot quick!

Lucy Shepherd
Ilfracombe CE Junior School, Ilfracombe

World Cup Fever

W hat! We are playing France
O wen what a goal
R ooney cannot make it
L ikely to win
D avid score a goal

C ome on Gerrard
U p to Heaven England
P eter Crouch missed a penalty

F ans go mad for England
E veryone hopes England will win
V ery good save
E veryone screams
R ed flags wave forever.

Jack Wilkinson (8)
Ilfracombe CE Junior School, Ilfracombe

World Cup Fever

W in that World Cup England
O wen I'm sure you can score a goal
R ooney get better we need you to play
L ions should be lucky so this time we can win
D on't miss the goal England we know you can do it

C ome on England you can do it
U p, up and away the ball goes in the air
P ut all your effort into it, we know you can do it

F ootball fans are clapping their hands in the air
E veryone wants England to win, win, win
V ersus Spain, versus Spain, England versus Spain
E ngland please win we have only won once
R ed and white flags waving in the air.

Sharna Embrey (8)
Ilfracombe CE Junior School, Ilfracombe

World Cup Fever

W ow, we're in the World Cup
O h it's so exciting
R ooney, Rooney
L ike it, love it, win it
D o your best

C ome on England
U p you go and win
P oland are losers, Poland are losers

F ootball, football
E ngland, England
V ersus Poland, versus Poland
E ngland, England
R eferees watching you.

Chloe Harmer (7)
Ilfracombe CE Junior School, Ilfracombe

World Cup Fever

W in England, win
O nly the World Cup is every four years
R ooney hope you play for Man United
L et Rooney play
D on't let us down

C ome on and win
U sually we should win
P arty all night

F or years
E ngland, England
V ictory win
E asily we should win
R un to shoot!

Freya Burnett (8)
Ilfracombe CE Junior School, Ilfracombe

World Cup Fever

W ow, I bet it's going to be cool
O n Saturday England please score
R ooney, Rooney we need you
L ights are going to shine like mad
D on't miss the goal

C ome on England
U kraine
P ick up your boots and score a goal

F ans are going to scream
E veryone is going to be excited in three days
V ersus
E ngland, you can do it
R obbo is the England goalkeeper.

Jazzie Pollard
Ilfracombe CE Junior School, Ilfracombe

World Cup Fever

W ow, England is good
O ld times' sake win that cup
R ooney get better
L ovely to see you win
D on't trip him up

C ome on England you have the world at your feet
U p to the pitch
P eter don't miss a goal

F ans cheer for England
E at my shorts Japan
V ery good goal
E veryone don't panic
R un to the goal.

James Uzzell (8)
Ilfracombe CE Junior School, Ilfracombe

World Cup Fever

W in England, win
O h, I hope you win England
R ooney do your best
L osers, Spain, losers
D on't lose England

C ould you win?
U p you come and do your best
P ut your back into it

F oot, you should do the work
E ngland win, England win
V ersus Spain, versus Spain
E ngland do what you have to do
R un for that ball.

Fern Pridmore
Ilfracombe CE Junior School, Ilfracombe

World Cup Fever

W orld Cup England win it
O wen get in there
R ooney come on
L ose it, never
D o it

C up is yours
U p to the Cup England
P ut up your heads

F ocus
E nough practise Rooney
V ictory is yours
E ngland win, England win
R ooney get in there.

Aidan Cooney (8)
Ilfracombe CE Junior School, Ilfracombe

World Cup Fever

W e want you to win England
O ld times' sake win that cup
R ooney's back in action
L earn football
D avid Beckham score a goal

C ome on England win that cup
U p the steps to the stadium
P laying football's great

F ans cheer and that's a fact
E at my shoes Germany
V ery good England
E ngland's very good at football
R un to the stadium or drive, don't walk.

Sammi Webster (7)
Ilfracombe CE Junior School, Ilfracombe

World Cup Fever

W e want England to win
O h, we're in the World Cup
R un and don't let yourselves down
L ennon, Lennon don't have a frown
D o your stuff

C an you do it England?
U p to the top England
P eter Crouch get to goal

F ans scream. scream, scream
E ngland get in there
V ote for England and they'll surely win
E ngland get in there
R obinson, do your goalkeeping!

Noah Turner (8)
Ilfracombe CE Junior School, Ilfracombe

World Cup Fever

W ow, I can't wait
O nly you can win this game
R emember you did it 40 years ago, you can do it again
L isten to the football song and sing along
D on't let us down, please

C ome on England, we know you can do it
U know what you have got to do
P lease England do your best

F orever, forever try your very best
E veryone's excited, they know you're going to win
V ersus any country you will win
E very day we want England to win
R ed and white, red and white, the England flag is red and white.

Rachel Beacham (8)
Ilfracombe CE Junior School, Ilfracombe

World Cup Fever

W in the World Cup England
O nly three more days to go
R ooney we hope your foot gets better
L et them win, let them win
D on't let us down England

C ome on England
U nderstand that they are going to win
P arty all night

F inally the day is coming
E ngland win, win, win, win
V ote for England
E ngland win
R un to shoot, run to shoot!

Caitlin Waters
Ilfracombe CE Junior School, Ilfracombe

World Cup Fever

W ow
O nly three days to go
R oar like a tiger
L ight up the pitch
D on't lose yourself

C ome on England
U ltra mad
P ut us in the semi

F inal
E veryone is roaring
V ote for England
E veryone
R oar!

Courtney Iles
Ilfracombe CE Junior School, Ilfracombe

World Cup Fever

W onderful news
O n Saturday it's the first match
R ed, blue, white are the colours of the England flag
L ace your shoes
D o think about what you are doing

C ome on England you can do it
U kraine is a country
P ull up as a team

F eel like you're going to win
E verybody is hoping you can win England
V ictory is coming soon
E verybody is cheering England
R obbo is the goalkeeper for England.

Sommer Ward (7)
Ilfracombe CE Junior School, Ilfracombe

World Cup Fever

W ow, you can do it
O n Saturday we've got to win
R ooney you've got to score a goal
L eave your worries behind
D on't give up England

C ome on England you can win
U se your skill
P lease don't let me down

F ootball fans are going to go crazy
E verybody is going to love it
V ictory for England
E ngland come on
R unning up and down the pitch!

Caitlin Blackmore da Silva (8)
Ilfracombe CE Junior School, Ilfracombe

World Cup Fever

W orld Cup every four years so come on England
O nly England should win
R ooney you might have broken your foot but don't give up
L ive football coming soon
D on't quit now

C up is the best trophy ever
U are the best ever team
P araguay are losers

F irst match 10th of June
E ngland you've got this far, don't give up now
V ery good, you've got to win the World Cup
E ngland, with the power you can win
R ooney is the best ever!

Eleanor Salfairso (8)
Ilfracombe CE Junior School, Ilfracombe

World Cup Fever

W orld Cup ready to be started, I am really excited
O w, wow! Go England go.
R oll England show us what you can do
L ively people ready to start
D on't kick that ball over there

C areful there, don't knock that cup
U there, you'll never win
P ut that trophy down

F irst time I've won the World Cup
E ngland, you can't give up now
V ery lively people on the pitch
E ngland with your power kick that ball
R you going to win because we hope you do!

Megan Hornsby (8)
Ilfracombe CE Junior School, Ilfracombe

World Cup Fever

W in, win England win
O h yes, carry on don't give up
R un England, run, run
L ess talking more playing
D on't stop England carry on

C ome on England stop messing about
U p there is the goal, shoot, shoot, shoot
P lay, play, you've got to play

F inal, it's the final, win it
E ngland, England, come on England, *England*
V ery good keep it up
E ngland, England, we support England
R un, run, run, run, run, England.

Leticia Collins (8)
Ilfracombe CE Junior School, Ilfracombe

Where Teachers Keep Their Pets

(Based on 'Where Teachers Keep their Pets' by Paul Cookson)

Mrs Slants had some ants
Kept them in her underpants.

Mr Cheese had wonderful bees
And kept them in his dungarees.

Mrs Sare has a white mare
And keeps it in her underwear.

Mr Mish has a fancy fish
It swims in a cat's dish.

Mrs Hoot had some scary newts
She kept them in her loud flute.

Mr Ten had a beautiful hen
Who lived in a messy pen.

Mrs Clark has a lovely lark
And flies it in a park.

Molly Kendall & Bethany Ward (8)
Manor CE School, Bristol

Football Crazy

Ronaldinho scored a goal, 'Goal!'
Beckham hit the pole, pole
Skill by Joe Cole, Cole
Henry kicked a bowl, bowl
Frank Lampard hurt his knee
Because he fell into a tree
Ronaldhino scored a goal, 'Goal!'
Beckham hit the pole, pole!
Skill by Joe Cole, Cole
Henry kicks a bowl, bowl!

Bethany Ward & Biel Casey (8)
Manor CE Primary School, Bristol

Where Teachers Keep Their Pets

(Based on 'Where Keep their Pets' by Paul Cookson)

Mrs Fittens has several kittens
And keeps them in her fluffy mittens.

Mrs Purl had a squirrel
Living in her curls.

Mrs Eade had a pet called Lead
Nesting in her nasty weed.

Mr Bear had a wondrous hare
Living in his underwear.

Mr Pog had a naughty dog
Lying in his horrible log.

Mrs Cox had a hungry fox
Living in her curly locks.

Mr Meer keeps a clever deer
Who bathes all day in his awful beer.

Mrs Pat had a ginger cat
Living under naked rats.

Mrs Funny has a smelly bunny
And it's always in her tummy.

Mrs Dare has a grizzly bear
Hiding in her comfy chair.

Mr Nee had a few nasty bees
Buzzing in his dungarees.

Miss Sale had a blue whale
Living in her pink tail.

Sophie Rose & Esther Haigh (8)
Manor CE Primary School, Bristol

Where Teachers Keep Their Pets

(Based on 'Where Teachers Keep their Pets' by Paul Cookson)

Mr Sunny has a funny bunny
Hiding in his tummy.

Mrs Clock has a furry flock
Hiding in her smelly sock.

Mr Fear has a brown deer
Living in his can of beer.

Mrs Clees had some buzzing bees
Hiding in her dungarees.

Mr Bangeroo has a wandering kangaroo
And keeps it down the loo!

Mr Knobbly Knees had some mysterious bees
Hiding in his lumpy peas.

Mrs Nat had a naught cat
Who lived under the old hat.

Ali Rostam-Shirazi, Biel Casey & Oliver Aldom (8)
Manor CE Primary School, Bristol

Isabel And The Fox

(Inspired by 'Adventures of Isabel' by Ogden Nash)

Isabel met an enormous fox
Isabel put the fox in the box.

The fox was hungry, the fox got out
The fox's big mouth was ready to shout.

The fox said, 'Isabel, I'll eat you up.'
And ran to get his plate and cup!

Isabel, Isabel got her knife
And attacked the fox to save her life.

The fox escaped and went to his den
Isabel left in search of a hen!

Alexander Monk (8) & Luke Bennett (7)
Manor CE Primary School, Bristol

What Is It Like?

What can I taste?
I can taste the cold bitter breeze
and sometimes I wonder how old the breeze is.

What can I smell?
I can smell the rough woody trees
and I feel a bit cold so I'm putting on my hoody.

What can I hear?
I can hear the birds squeaking and singing
and now I can hear the crazy frog dinging away.

What can I see?
I can see the cold salty sea
and once I tasted a pea and I hated it.

What can I feel?
I can feel the pen I'm holding to write this poem.

Phoenix Hudson (8)
St Ives Junior School, St Ives

My Five Senses

I took and felt the crispy moss in the palm of my hand
I heard the amazing, twittering, squawking, whistling
Cheeping, humming, croaking of the birds
I smelt the fresh, sweet-smelling green grass wafting up my nose
I saw amazing bark on the trees
I tasted the dry grass scattered over the field.

Kelsey Foster (9)
St Ives Junior School, St Ives

A Walk In The Garden

The sight I can see is the question you are asking me.
What colour is that crow?
Black, black as ebony.
What colour is the sky?
Baby-blue and so are you.
What do all the birds sound like?
Like angels singing high above the sky
Humming, chirping, whistling too.
I can smell. What do you smell?
I can smell the salty air wafting from the sea.
I can smell blossoming pink flowers
I can touch. What can you touch?
I can touch the delicate twigs falling from the trees.

Georgia Trodd (9)
St Ives Junior School, St Ives

The Breezy Summer's Day

What does it smell like?
It smells like the fresh summer's air.
What colour is it?
It is sparkling green and muddy brown.
What does it taste like?
It tastes fresh.
What does it sound like?
It sounds like swaying and calm.
What does it look like?
It looks enchanted.
What does it feel like?
It feels like you can relax.
Can you guess what it is?
It is a summer's day.

Jessica Baxendale (9)
St Ives Junior School, St Ives

The Eagle

The black and gold eagle
Swooping down, slicing his prey
With sharp talons
His prey is a mouse
Long and fearsome teeth
Sink deep into his prey
But when the eagle has bad weather
He goes home to sleep from midday to midnight.

Ryan Clewer-Wolk (8)
St Ives Junior School, St Ives

A Warm Summer's Day

The sky is moving slowly downstream
The sea is calm today
I can smell the beautiful air
I can feel the sun on my back
The sweat running down my spine
I can see the trees moving around and around
I can hear the birds singing around my friends and I.

Nicole Jenkins (9)
St Ives Junior School, St Ives

One Summer's Day

I could smell lavender, swishing and swashing left and right.
I could hear the swirling of the lake as my dog jumped into the water.
I could see old rotting trees all orange and soft with age.
I could touch the bark and it would dissolve underneath my fingers.
I could taste the sweet air blowing into my face.
That was my walk on a summer's day.

Jed Parker (9)
St Ives Junior School, St Ives

Summer Senses

As I walked across the green grass
I heard the crunching of the leaves under my feet
The dark sky soon turned light
I saw the blue sky peeking through the clouds
Trees were moving left and right
I could feel the warm summer air
It soon turned cold and it was night
I could smell the wet damp grass.

Jack Knipe (9)
St Ives Junior School, St Ives

One Summer's Day

I hear seagulls squawking above the golden sand.
I see them diving downwards into the deep blue ocean.
I taste the sweet salty air on the tip of my tongue.
I feel the lovely warm sand on my hands.
I smell the delicious fish and chips in our hands.

Bradley Babb (9)
St Ives Junior School, St Ives

Make The Garden Smell

The garden smells of light blue salty sea air
I can see working men chattering to each other
I can hear footprints of the birds
I can feel dark brown wood
I can taste the breeze in all directions
I can feel oxygen entering my brain
I am feeling thrilled in my beloved mind
I am seeing things in my mind
I am thinking of flowers growing fresh
I am thinking faintly.

Molly Young (8)
St Ives Junior School, St Ives

My Senses

I can hear the birds rustling in the dark green pine cone trees.
I can see the bugs crawling through the luscious grass.
I can feel the cool breeze on my hands.
I can taste the lovely, fresh, cool air on the tip of my tongue.
I can smell the trees' fresh bark.

Steven Cooper (9)
St Ives Junior School, St Ives

The Sweet Green Field

The beautiful robin dives not very high off the ground
Crows waddle like penguins
Birds sing lullabies
The air taste like sweets pouring into my mouth
The smell is the fresh green grass.

Liam Pugh (9)
St Ives Junior School, St Ives

The Magic Door

As I crept through a magic door
I saw the most beautiful sight
A dragon and a knight were having a most terrible fight.

I really could not stop myself
So I let out a shout
The knight's dark cold sword hit it
And blood came pouring out.

I woke up . . .
I think it was a nightmare . . .
But I'm not sure.

Ethan Carney (9)
St Ives Junior School, St Ives

Old Farm

I can see the rusty window sills flapping round the farm
I can smell rotten hay and smell old tractor fuel
I can feel a falling apart tractor
I can hear the floorboards falling down onto the windows and hear
the windows smashing
Will they ever build it again?
Will anybody ever live there again?

Christopher Hosking (9)
St Ives Junior School, St Ives

Summer Senses

I can see wood, white, yellow and brown
I can smell roast dinner cooking in the infants' school
I can hear birds singing kindly
The clouds are hazy and white
I feel warm, happy and cheerful.

Ryan Wiggin (9)
St Ives Junior School, St Ives

Skating

I can see loads of people on skateboards
I can hear people shout, 'Move out of my way!'
I get a shock because it is a good trick
And I can smell burning metal
I can taste fresh air.

Karl Sweet (9)
St Ives Junior School, St Ives

The Calm Nature

What does it taste like?
I can taste the texture of the calm, swaying breeze.
What does it smell like?
I can smell the calm fresh sea air.
I can smell freshly made roast dinner.
What does it feel like?
I can feel the silky green grass.
I can feel the calm, swaying breeze on my peachy skin.
What does it look like?
I can see the calm, swaying nature.
I can see the calm, swaying sea.
What does it sound like?
I can hear little children playing swiftly.

Danielle Rudkin (8)
St Ives Junior School, St Ives

The Magic Mirror

When I looked in the magic mirror
I saw an ugly dragon
But it was so ugly I could not bear to look at it.

When I leapt into the magic mirror
I was stranded on a desert island
The island was surrounded and full of monsters
So I went back into the magic mirror.

When I looked into the mirror for the second time
I saw an *alien* coming for me.

Suddenly *ring, ring, ring,* I woke up
The magic mirror lay beside my bed
Was it a dream?

Darcy Payton-Barnard (8)
St Ives Junior School, St Ives

Love

Love is the colour of the sun
It smells like chocolates
It is like a rose in the sky - at sunset.

Love feels like touching a cloud
So gentle.

But it can be soft or strong
And love can be so brief - or love can be so long!

Liza Mazzotta (10)
St Ursula's High School, Bristol

Titanic

The great Queen of the Ocean
The Pride of the White Star Line

This ship is so vast
A ship of dreams

Now at the bottom of the ocean.

I weep for loved ones
Asleep forever in the Titanic.

Juliet Owens (9)
St Ursula's High School, Bristol

Monkeys!

Monkeys swinging in a line,
From branch to branch - vine to vine.
They eat bananas which they love,
Under the blue skies far above.

Andreas Aristotelous (11)
St Ursula's High School, Bristol

Ballet Class

You grab the clips
You snatch the spray
You put them all together
And there's your bun.
You struggle on your tights
You slip on your leotard
You pull on your shoes
And run into class.

The beat of the music makes you want to dance
You warm up at the barre
You spin, you twirl
You spring in your sautés
You run to the front in the révérence
When it's time to go you think, *no, no, no!*
Your feet just itch to continue
You just don't want to stop dancing.

Philippa Hyde (10)
St Ursula's High School, Bristol

The Garden Of Eden

Lots of lovely flowers
All kinds of animals
Fruits of all sorts
Paradise on Earth.

Slithering serpent
Leading Eve astray
Tricked her
Made her taste the apple.

Eve persuaded Adam,
'Try this tasty fruit.'
God was disappointed
That they had disobeyed.

Out of the Garden they ran
Away from paradise on Earth.

Alex Saliveros (10)
St Ursula's High School, Bristol

Shark!

Slicing through the sea
Hunting its prey!

Attacking!

Ripping!

Devouring all in its way
There's blood in the spray!

Jonathan Hulin (11)
St Ursula's High School, Bristol

A Sweet Meadow

One day I went out walking
But then I lost my way
I was in a meadow
Shining in the day.
Full of flowers and rabbits galore
A place of beauty, for even the poor.

I saw a cross
And knelt to pray
To thank God for this perfect day.

Shannon Pincott (9)
St Ursula's High School, Bristol

A Beautiful Sunset

As I was walking across a field
I saw a cross and then kneeled.

I said my prayers
To the Lord, who cares.

I then walked on
But not for long.

I saw the sunset
And could not carry on.

I thanked the Lord for the huge orange sun
I whispered goodbye - and then it was gone.

So now it is night
And I pray for the light.

Rebecca Hale (9)
St Ursula's High School, Bristol

God's World

Nature is beautiful
All over the world
Full of flowers, trees and fruit!
Nature is everywhere
God made our world for us to enjoy
Birds hopping from tree to tree
Deer running through flowers.

Nature is in the sea
It has the biggest and smallest creatures
It has plants and coral
The sea is beautiful but also dangerous
It has the most dangerous creature
The sea has colourful and beautiful fish.

Billy Rigg (10)
St Ursula's High School, Bristol

The Forest

Light brown pine needles on the big shady forest floor
Flexible but frail, the green grass stood everywhere
Tall trees stand high up in the warm air
But somehow ants can climb right to the top
Small creatures hidden by the leaf litter
Waiting for an insect smaller than it.

Tristan Garrett (9)
Sandford Primary School, Crediton

Extraordinary Leaves

Crispy leaves on the bed in the forest of the farm
All the flaky coloured leaves swirling swiftly up the sloping hills
They make a faint whisper as quiet as a mouse
The smell of earth and moss brushes your face when the
gentle breeze blows
But altogether it's just extraordinary!

Liam Adams (9)
Sandford Primary School, Crediton

The Unfortunate Caterpillar (Clive)

A fat juicy caterpillar basking on a leaf
Little does he know that there's an ant underneath
As the purple wriggler wiggles along
He realises something's wrong
The ant starts crawling up the leaf
It clicks its pincers as if a sheath
Then grabs poor Clive around the head
And in one slice
Clive is dead!

Noah Parker (10)
Sandford Primary School, Crediton

Woodland Poem

Short sharp grass swaying softly in the middle of the forest
Covering the bumpy ground
How it got there no one will know
Down on the rocky ground, where stomping feet land
The ants are marching back to their big bulky nest where
their queen lies
Off they go again to get more supplies to build up the nest
They never stop for any rests!

Charlotte Ward (9)
Sandford Primary School, Crediton

The Silly Alphabet

A is for apple, very tasty
B is for bun, got to be hasty
C is for cat, they scratch like mad
D is for dog, they are sometimes bad
E is for elephant very, very big
F is for frog, dancing a jig
G is for grizzly, running around
H is for heffalump, falling to the ground
I is for iguana climbing trees
J is for jaguar falling on his knees
K is for koala eating leaves
L is for lion stalking the eaves
M is for mouse in his little hole
N is for nest up the pole
O is for oval as round as can be
P is for person, as most of us can see
Q is for quill, writing with your hand
R is for rap in the band
S is for skiing, sliding down the slope
T is for topping, look there's the Pope
U is for underground, using the light
V is for vase, planting at night
W is for wellies, getting all wet
X is for xylophone, catching with a net
Y is for yak, winding down the window
Z is for zebra being all silly.

Sarah Tucker (9)
Sandford Primary School, Crediton

My Cat

I have a cat
A tabby cat
My cat is not very fat
My cat likes catching birds and mice
My cat is not very nice
She likes eating meat from tins
If she doesn't like it
We throw it in the bin
That's all now
Goodbye I say
Please come and call another day!

Ellie Balsdon (9)
Sandford Primary School, Crediton

School

S hh, the lesson began
C an't see why we can't talk
H ate it, hate it, it sucks so bad
O h, oh, I can't take it anymore
O h why school, why do you exist?
L eave me alone, I'm sick of you!

Verity Potts (9)
Sandford Primary School, Crediton

My Young Horse

M y riding teacher is really bossy
'Y ou get your heels down,' she shouts

'Y our heels aren't down'
O h dear, somebody help me
U h oh, here she comes with the whip
'N aughty Sylvester,' she screams
'G et him moving Vicky'

H ere we go again
O h Sylvester no, no, no
R iiiipppp
S creams echoed off the stables
'E hh Miss Hazel! You've got a hole in your trousers.'

Vicky Pullen (9)
Sandford Primary School, Crediton

Mammals

You see them scuttle across the ground
You see them leap and jump around
Some are common, some are rare
But most are given good care
Have you got it yet?
Yes, they're mammals.

Kai Dudley (9)
Sandford Primary School, Crediton

The Alphabet Poem

A is for ant, nice and small
B is for bumbling while entering the hall
C is for can, which I find hard to open
D is for dog, which you buy with a token
E is for elephant, really *big*
F is for frog, dancing a jig
G is for Granny, all old and bony
H is for heffalump, although it's a phoney
I is for ink which is very messy
J is for jelly which I named Bessy
K is for king, very royal
L is for light which is made out of foil
M is for mouse all jumpy and squeaky
N is for night-time, which is very, very *freaky*
O is for oak which grows to a height
P is for person which gets in a fight
Q is for queen prancing around
R is for rabbit on the ground
S is for snake which is very, very scaly
T is for tea which I have daily
U is for umbrella which shelters us from rain
V is vicar who travels by train
W is wet all over the place
X is xylophone which I play on my face
Y is yak, very, very hairy
Z is for zebra who is a very, very funny fairy!

Gemma MacIntyre (9)
Sandford Primary School, Crediton

Mr Waterfall

Dear Mr Waterfall
May I sit in your pool?
Dear Mr Waterfall
Your water's frothy, bubbly too
Dear Mr Waterfall
It's warm out here and you're cold and cool
Dear Mr Waterfall
You're light and foamy
White like . . .
. . . Toffee.

Ami Maya (8)
Sandford Primary School, Crediton

People

People can be good and fun when they are nice to everyone
People can be bright and beautiful but they have to be good
to other people
You should try to involve everyone and then you will have lots of fun
So there you go, I have told you some stuff, I hope you will use
it very much.

Josie-Lee Godwin (10)
Two Mile Hill Junior School, Bristol

All Day Plan

Go to sleep
Wake up
Get dressed
Have breakfast
Off to school
Break up
Make up
Into class
Out to play
Bell rings
Back inside
Have lunch
Yum-yum
Back outside
Mess about
Annoy the teachers
Get told off
Start to cry
Back in class
Saying sorry
End of the day
Out of school
Back home
Have tea
Back to bed
Next day
Don't go to school
Which I hate.

Shannon Baker (10)
Two Mile Hill Junior School, Bristol

My Noisy Budgie

My budgie is so noisy
He wakes up everybody.

My budgie is so naughty
People complain.

My budgie makes so much noise
That a big green fly comes.

My budgie is big
No animal touches it.

My budgie is loud
I ask my mum what will make him shut up.

My budgie is not loud
When he's asleep.

Sunny Singh (10)
Two Mile Hill Junior School, Bristol

World Cup

W ill we win the World Cup
O r maybe someone else?
R ooney's out without a doubt
L oving our country for who we are
D on't you know the cup's gonna go

C ome and watch our team win
U s together, we can win
P elé had a gold, but he is old.

Joe Haskins (10)
Two Mile Hill Junior School, Bristol

Ice Cream

Ice cream is cold, it always makes me shiver
I like to eat it by the river
I eat it in the summer
As does my little brother
It smells like sweet and sour
And so does a little flower
When it rains I take it into the shower
It fills me with laughter.

Hannah-May Ash (8)
Two Mile Hill Junior School, Bristol

Night Sky

Night skies are dark and cold
But the stars light it up wherever you go
You will always see the snow come down from above.

In the dark you will see animals running around
On the ground down under the sky I wonder if you know
That the stars will let everything go.

Night skies are beautiful and shiny, so look above
And see the stars glitter all around you.

Rhianna Pursey (9)
Two Mile Hill Junior School, Bristol

England!

All the players in the hall, nervously waiting to play football!
Out runs Beckham, followed by Rooney
Because of the sight, the crowd are going loony.

They get into their positions, all ready and waiting
About to play the team they've always been hating.

It's come to half-time, it's 2-1 to Brazil
Sad and upset is how England feel.

Back to the game, England's on a roll
Owen's got the ball, hang on, I think it's a *goal!*

The game is now over and who's won the cup?
England of course, *na na na na na*
And Ronaldinho says, '*Shut up.*'

Monique Ash (10)
Two Mile Hill Junior School, Bristol

Professional Footballer

I am a professional footballer
I am a skilful footballer
I am a funny kid
I am a hungry child
I am a fun chum
I am a silky sock
I am a strong boy
I am a Duracel battery which never runs out.

Thomas Williams (10)
Two Mile Hill Junior School, Bristol

What The Sun Is

The sun is a pile of gold waiting to be spent
The sun is a golden sword waiting to be fought with
The sun is a golden dog waiting to be stroked
The sun is a golden book waiting to be read
The sun is a golden yolk from an egg
The sun is a yellow pot of paint waiting to be painted with
The sun is a golden ball waiting to be hit
The sun is a golden door waiting to be opened
The sun is a golden frame waiting for something to go in it
The sun is a chair waiting to be sat on
The sun is a golden rubber waiting to rub out
The sun is a yellow clock waiting to tell the time
The sun is a golden piece of paper waiting to be written on.

Tristan White (10)
Two Mile Hill Junior School, Bristol

The Seasons Of The Year

T here are four seasons in the year
H owever they bring nothing to fear
E ach has a special name

S ummer is the hottest, it gets hotter as it nears
E veryone can have a treat, the ice cream man is here
A utumn comes after it and the leaves fall off the trees
S ummer's disappeared and hayfever won't make you sneeze
O ncoming is the winter, the temperature has gone cold
N ext it will be snowing, that's what we've been told
S pring is straight after, there's blossom on the trees

O ne season has three months
F or there are twelve months in a year

T rue I'm sure I am
H ence everybody knows
E xtraordinary they are different, every single time

Y early this will happen
E ach and every one
A nd all people know this well
R egularly (every year) this routine is complete
And it goes by the name of *The Seasons Of The Year.*

Joshua Tiley (10)
Two Mile Hill Junior School, Bristol

Down In The Valley

Down in the valley where the green grass grows
There was a squirrel and a flower and a big red rose.

The next day when I went down into the valley where the
green grass grows
I saw a crocodile without any toes.

So I asked the croc, 'Where is the squirrel and the flower and
the big red rose?'
But he just said, 'Nobody knows.'

So I searched down low and I searched up high
But guess where I found them, in the sky.

Jasmine Gee (10)
Two Mile Hill Junior School, Bristol

Life

Life is full of ups and downs,
Life could be full of misery and frowns,
But one thing's for sure, I'm *glad* to say,
Life could be cleared of yesterday.

To say I'm not sick would just be a dream,
Just like a chocolate brownie covered in cream,
It sounds so delicious, life also can be,
Just make the most of life and sun you shall see.

Life is like a precious gem, meant for all women and men,
Treasure your life, happy you should be
And let all your troubles wash out in the sea.

Georgina Anderson (10)
Two Mile Hill Junior School, Bristol

Lunchtimes

Can you tell me, if you please
Who it is that likes mushy peas?
Louise likes mushy peas.
How about Sam?
Sam likes ham.
How about Millie?
Millie likes chilli.
How about Jean?
Jean likes beans.
How about Hollie?
Hollie likes lollies.
How about Jake?
Jake likes cakes.
How about Ross?
Ross likes candyfloss.
Hey, what about Catherine Babalab?
Well, she goes home for lunch!

Hannah Gunningham (10)
Two Mile Hill Junior School, Bristol

Lions

Lions are lazy, they like to lounge around
They look like a fantastic furry ball prancing up and down
Lions are furious and fiery when they catch their prey
Because when they do they say hip hip hooray
They fight all day, they fight all night
So all the others get a fright
These are some of their favourite things
But most of all they love to . . . *roar!*

Josie Marks (10)
Two Mile Hill Junior School, Bristol

Two Mile Hill's Teachers

Miss Bindon wears colourful bindis that hang off her hair
And loop onto her forehead
Miss Gathercole gathers lots of coal in the winter
And saves it all for the summer to have a barbecue.
Mr Long is long and thin which he enjoys
As he can pick delicious fruits from high trees.
Miss Ward in the morning is always standing in front of the wardrobe
Fussing about what to wear.
Miss Barton is always trying to act like Bart Simpson
Skateboarding to school from Barton Hill.

Saira Ali (10)
Two Mile Hill Junior School, Bristol

I Am A . . .

I am a slithery slimy snake slithering around
I am a lanky lofty lion prancing around
I am a dopey downright, dirty, dog always on watch
I am a helpful happy horse racing for glory
I am cheerful chubby children playing around
I am a funny flabby fish swimming around
I am a popular pink pig snorting around.

Jack Holbrook (10)
Two Mile Hill Junior School, Bristol

The Sun

The sun is an orange, sweet and juicy.
It is a yellow beach ball kicked high into the sky.
It is a gold coin flicked into the air.
It is a yellow boat floating calmly across the still sea.
It is the yellow light from the stars in the night sky.
It is a gold bottle top floating in a puddle.
It is a smiling face looking down on us all.

Isaac Wise (10)
Two Mile Hill Junior School, Bristol

My Friends

One of my mates is Jack
In football Liam likes to hack
Liam is my best mate
For school James is late.

Andrew is a cool dude
He loves talking about food
He's computer mad
But he's naughty and bad.

My best mate is Liam
He never stops laughing
In maths he's good at halving
Liam is so good at maths.

Then there's me, the last one
I am the most fun
I am the best of them all
Always breaking the law.

Alex Millard (9)
Two Mile Hill Junior School, Bristol

Rabbits

Rabbits are cute
Rabbits jump around
Rabbits are soft

Rabbits are funny
Rabbits are fast
Rabbits race around

Rabbits are cosy
Rabbits are nice
What more can you ask for?

Ikram Omar (9)
Two Mile Hill Junior School, Bristol

The Ocean

The ocean is a prowling cat pouncing on the seashore sand
The ocean is a mere copy of the sky but upside down
with no fluffy clouds
The ocean is a roaring lion moving through the night
The ocean is a careful mother homing small sea creatures
The ocean is a big bear, big and strong
The ocean is invisible, it will never die
The ocean will always be there.

Lewis Bolley (10)
Two Mile Hill Junior School, Bristol

My Friends

One of my mates is Jack
He is my best friend
Another mate is James
He is late in school.

Alex sometimes fights
Liam plays football
I chill along in school
Me and my friends do it all.

We are all the best of friends
We always try our hardest
To do our work in class
And stay the best of friends.

Andrew Hughes (10)
Two Mile Hill Junior School, Bristol

Kittens

Kittens are cute
Kittens are funny
Kittens race around the house

Kittens are strange
Kittens jump around
They stretch by the fire.

Kittens are cosy
Kittens are playful
What more could you ask for?

Hannah Rumble (10)
Two Mile Hill Junior School, Bristol

The BFFL Poem

Friends are for life
Friends are forever
Friends for the future
Having friends is so clever.

Playing games
And having lots of fun
Of course my best friend
Is always my mum.

Holidays, birthdays, Christmas as well
Laughing and talking with stories to tell
Sleeping at my friend's house
All the time staying up till nine.

Friends are so good, fun and great
They laugh around with me
Which I hate.

Paige Groves (10)
Two Mile Hill Junior School, Bristol

Dolphins

Dolphins are beautiful
Dolphins are cute
Dolphins are funny
Dolphins are wonderful
Dolphins are greedy
Dolphins are lively
Dolphins are messy and fun
Dolphins are noisy
Dolphins are sweet and kind
Dolphins have feelings too.

Molly Shortman (9)
Two Mile Hill Junior School, Bristol

My Family

My nan is a bat because she stays up
All night but stays asleep all day.

My dad is an ox because he is super strong
My mum is a leopard because she's always running around for us.

My sister is a snake because she's very sly
My other sister is a lion because she's always having fights.

My next sister is a bear because she likes jam
My last sister is a mouse because she is so quiet and also squeaks
And I'm a monkey because I'm the funniest and cheekiest of them all.

James Broad (9)
Two Mile Hill Junior School, Bristol

Sun And Moon

Sun is a gold medal shining in the sky
Moon is a silver plate with half of a pie
Sun shines like a round beach ball
Moon is a huge snowball
Sun is very bright
Moon is quite dull and almost out of sight
Sun is very hot in the summer holidays
Moon is cold in the winter holidays.

Saif Majid (10)
Two Mile Hill Junior School, Bristol

The Storm

Thunder crushing the air
Lightning flashing everywhere
The noise making people scared
People hiding under their beds
Trying to escape from this terrible noise
But they can't escape
And the storm still torments the sky.

George Gould (9)
Two Mile Hill Junior School, Bristol

Holiday

My holiday was great
My holiday was fun
My holiday was hot, hotter than ever
My holiday was full of happiness, it was the best
My holiday was fantastic
What was yours like?

Karampreet Kour (10)
Two Mile Hill Junior School, Bristol

Who Likes Mushy Peas?

Can you tell me please
Who likes mushy peas?
Louise likes peas.
How about Bob?
Bob likes cod.
How about Hellen?
Hellen likes melon.
How about Dan?
Dan likes ham.
How about Holly?
Holly likes lollies.
How about Jake?
Jake likes cake.
Stop!
Just tell me, who likes mushy peas?

Charlie Lovell (10)
Two Mile Hill Junior School, Bristol

I Am, I Am

I am, I am a monkey that swings through the trees
I am, I am a giraffe eating lots of leaves
I am, I am a rhino that's got a sharp nose
I am, I am a hamster that did a little pose.

Harrison Bush (9)
Two Mile Hill Junior School, Bristol

Two Little Monkeys

Two little monkeys fighting in bed
One fell out and hit his head
The other called the doctor
And the doctor said,
'That is what you get for fighting in bed.'

Rownita Marston (8)
Two Mile Hill Junior School, Bristol

My Friends

I have friends that always laugh
They're also very helpful when they take my book
And put it in the box
Whenever they are around me we always scream and shout
They always see me home because we play about
I see them home and then we always shout
And those are my friends.

Jordan Clark (9)
Two Mile Hill Junior School, Bristol

Seasons

Winter is cold and it's snowy
Spring is sunny and it's Easter
In autumn the leaves fall off the trees
In summer bees and wasps are ready to sting
And you can have a barbecue, you can have ice cream
In winter it's Christmas and Jesus is born
In summer ice creams are ready to eat
In spring you watch TV
In autumn you watch the fireworks
Seasons - which one is it now?

Daniel Currell (8)
Two Mile Hill Junior School, Bristol

Chocolate

Chocolate makes me feel good on a rainy night
Every night I have a bite I might tonight
My mum would like a bite
But I'm going to fight.

Lewis Willett (8)
Two Mile Hill Junior School, Bristol

My Pets

I have hundreds and thousands of pets
I have cats and dogs, guinea pigs and hamsters
How about chinchillas or tarantulas?

I have hundreds and thousands of pets
I have lions, tigers, frogs and flies
Have you ever heard of toads and spiders?

I have hundreds and thousands of pets
Beetles, bugs, dolphins and whales
What about octopus and fish?

I have hundreds and thousands of pets
You are probably wondering how I manage
I don't have to
They are not all mine.

Rebecca Marks (9)
Two Mile Hill Junior School, Bristol

Noise

The colour's red
It feels like madness
It smells like a dump
It sounds horrible.

Ross Morgan (8)
Ubley CE Primary School, Bristol

The Moon

The colour is yellow
It feels like a meal of cheese
It smells like warm soup
It tastes like cheese
It sounds like fairies
It looks like a big shiny ball!

Flora Chamberlain (8)
Ubley CE Primary School, Bristol

Fear

The colour is blood-red
It feels like a dead body
It smells like blood
It tastes like a salty crisp
It sounds like a silenced graveyard
It looks like a vampire bat.

Abigail Lambert (9)
Ubley CE Primary School, Bristol

Air

The colour is sparkling white
It feels like a yellow bird flying through the sky
It smells like fresh roses in the summer
It tastes like a bunch of tulips
It sounds like birds tweeting in the sky
It looks like blue and white peace.

Callum Aldridge (8)
Ubley CE Primary School, Bristol

Fire

The colour is orange
It feels like hot things
It smells like flames
It tastes like oranges
It sounds like crackling logs
It looks like an orange light.

Georgia Buxton (8)
Ubley CE Primary School, Bristol

Happiness

The colour is pink
It feels like a field of flowers
It smells like a red rose
It tastes like sweets
It sounds like children playing
It looks like a play area.

Charlotte Fear (7)
Ubley CE Primary School, Bristol